THE BOOK BORROW BOOK

THIS BOOK BELONGS TO:

_____

BOOK	BORROWER	DATE

BOOK	BORROWER	DATE

BOOK	BORROWER	DATE

BOOK	BORROWER	DATE

BOOK	BORROWER	DATE

BOOK	BORROWER	DATE

BOOK	BORROWER	DATE

BOOK	BORROWER	DATE

BOOK	BORROWER	DATE

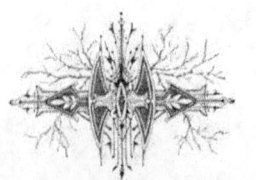

BOOK	BORROWER	DATE

BOOK	BORROWER	DATE

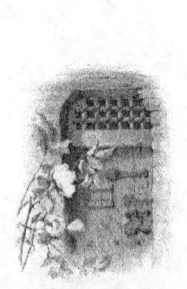

BOOK	BORROWER	DATE

BOOK	BORROWER	DATE

BOOK	BORROWER	DATE

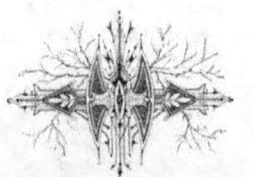

BOOK	BORROWER	DATE

BOOK	BORROWER	DATE

BOOK	BORROWER	DATE

BOOK	BORROWER	DATE

BOOK	BORROWER	DATE

BOOK	BORROWER	DATE

BOOK	BORROWER	DATE

BOOK	BORROWER	DATE

BOOK	BORROWER	DATE

BOOK	BORROWER	DATE

USE THIS SPACE TO KEEP A LIST OF PEOPLE WITH OVERDUE BOOKS

HANDY TIP!

If, in your efforts to get your book returned, you happen to get blood on the pages, there's an easy solution.

Mix half a cup of white vinegar with half a cup of water (make sure the vinegar you use is completely clear).

Moisten a cotton ball with the solution and carefully dab the affected area.

IF YOU BORROW MY BOOK AND DON'T RETURN IT

You pay the price.

www.ingramcontent.com/pod-product-compliance
Lightning Source LLC
Chambersburg PA
CBHW072102290426
44110CB00014B/1784